becoming
— a —
designer
— of —
distinction

becoming
a
designer
of
distinction

what interior design
school won't teach you

tabitha evans

BMcTALKS Press
4980 South Alma School Road
Suite 2-493
Chandler, Arizona 85248

Copyright © 2020 by Tabitha Evans. All rights reserved.

No part of this publication may be reproduced in any form beyond the copying permitted by US Copyright Law, Section 107, "fair use" in teaching or research, Section 108, certain library copying, or in published media by reviewers in limited excerpts; stored in a retrieval system; or transmitted in any form or by any means, electronic, mechanical, photocopying, recording, scanning, or otherwise without the prior written permission of the Publisher. Requests to the Publisher for permissions should be submitted to the Permissions Department, BMcTALKS Press, 4980 S. Alma School Road, Ste 2-493, Chandler, AZ 85248 or at www.bmctalkspress.com/permissions

Disclaimer: This book is for educational purposes only. The views expressed are those of the author alone and should not be taken as expert instruction or commands. The reader is responsible for his or her own actions. Adherence to all applicable laws and regulations, including international, federal, state, and local governing professional licensing, business practices, advertising, and all other aspects of doing business in the United States, Canada, or any other jurisdiction is the sole responsibility of the purchaser or reader. Neither the author nor the publisher assumes any responsibility or liability whatsoever on the behalf of the purchaser or reader of these materials.

The views expressed in this publication are those of the author; are the responsibility of the author; and do not necessarily reflect or represent the views of BMcTALKS Press, its owner, or its contractors.

Volume pricing is available to bulk orders placed by corporations, associations, and others. For details, please contact BMcTALKS Press at info@bmtpress.com

FIRST EDITION

Library of Congress Control Number: 2020912859

ISBN: 978-1-7351192-6-7 (paperback)
ISBN: 978-1-7351192-7-4 (eBook)

Printed in the United States of America.

Dedication

This book is dedicated to all who strive to create something truly special.

Contents

Foreword **ix**
Introduction **xi**

1 **Authenticity:** It's What Sets You Apart! **1**
2 **Education:** It's Where You Learn **9**
3 **Volunteerism:** It's Who You Help **19**
4 **Mentorship:** It's Who You Mentor and Who Mentors You **25**
5 **Networking:** It's Who You Know **31**
6 **Work:** It's Where You Work, Earn, and Learn **37**
7 **Experience:** It's Where You Get Your Hands Dirty! **43**
8 **Strengths:** It's What You're Good At! **49**
9 **Recognition:** It's Where You Get Noticed **55**
10 **Communication:** It's How You Express Yourself **61**
11 **Positivity:** It's How You Ensure You're On! **69**
12 **Relatability:** It's When You Put Yourself in Their Shoes … Not Literally, of Course! **73**
13 **Protection:** It's How You Put Safeguards in Place **77**
14 **Workbook:** It's What Inspires, Drives, and Motivates You to Be the Best You Can Be in Interior Design **85**

About the Author **89**

Foreword

It was 2015 when I met Tabitha Evans. She impressed me with her undeniable ability to capture my attention with her beauty and remarkable talents as an interior designer. I soon discovered her many unique qualities, but at the top the list was her strong willingness to give of herself completely. Tabitha has an undeniably remarkable story. To say Tabitha is accomplished is an understatement. Tabitha has fought for our country, built a successful interior design firm, travels the country with a focus on senior living and multi-family housing, all the while raising a beautiful family of three wonderful kids alongside her film maker husband. Her desire to want to share her experiences and wisdom gained along the way with her peers makes this book a must-read.

Tabitha is involved in her design community, maximizes her connections to help it grow, and is enriched through her philanthropic causes. It goes without saying when Tabitha asked me to write the forward for her book that's focused on helping interiors designers gain enriching insight into their businesses, I was honored. Not only will this book be meaningful and a source of motivation, you will also have the opportunity to learn from a seasoned, well trained, and humble interior designer. I feel the stories within this book give us a glimpse into Tabitha's world and her inspiring teachings that are enriching and thoughtful. Through-out, you will be encouraged, inspired, and motivated and you will find wisdom that you can translate into your own firm and your own brand to create inspiring, energetic, and loving spaces for others to hold close to their lives.

May you find tranquility and inspiration in the notion of doing something kind and to be generous with your spirit for others just like Tabitha has within this beautiful body of work.

Dwayne Clark
Management expert and industry veteran with 25+ years of interior design experience

Introduction

In 2007 . . .

I started my career as an interior designer. It was one of the best decisions I have ever made. I have learned so much by diving right in and going for it. I know not everyone is as adventurous as me, nor do most people have the incredible support system I have had.

I have the support of my incredible husband, Matt, and parents on both sides of the family. I have three children and without Grandma's support, this would have been way harder. I also had an opportunity to find an amazing mentor right out of the gate who has shared a wealth of knowledge with me. She is now a dear friend who still shares incredible insights.

In this book, I want to share some of my lessons learned along the way to offer a hip way of informing people what they need to do to help pave the way to a successful career in interior design. In a sense, I want to give back and offer some guidance or mentorship for anyone who needs it and give readers the "wings" they need to fly.

The central theme of this book is to assist interior design enthusiasts to get to the next level, using a step-by-step guide, if you will, to find the interior designer inside the reader. My hope is for readers to create a more meaningful career through building a strong foundation of support and focusing on their strengths.

All my best,
Tabitha

Chapter 1

Authenticity

It's What Sets You Apart!

Authenticity can sound complicated but, it isn't. It is really quite simple.

DEFINITION
>au·then·tic·i·ty
>/ˌôTHenˈtisədē/
>noun
>[1]the quality of being authentic. "the paper should have established the authenticity of the documents before publishing them."
>[2]synonyms: genuineness, originality; rightfulness, legitimacy, legality, validity, bona fides "the authenticity of the painting" reliability, dependability, trustworthiness, truth, veracity, verity, faithfulness, fidelity, authoritativeness, credibility; accuracy, factualness; historicity; rare veridicality
>
>—Lexico.com

It's being Y-O-U. It's not copying others. Using others for inspiration is fine, however, why not create you? Be the creator of your own visions, ideas, and projects. Authenticity is what separates you from everyone else.

When you are genuine, other people will pick up on it. Use your own life experiences to guide you. It is okay to be different and is actually preferred, in many cases. When you get hired for a job, whoever hires you will be hiring you for what you offer, not for what you can copy from others. Keep that in mind and watch yourself for self-doubt. Your originality will make you shine!

Authenticity goes further than just projects and work. It's also Y-O-U and how you appear to others. How do you think you appear to others? How do want to appear to others? Have you ever pretended to be someone or something that you are not?

Eradicate those false pretenses, and be who you were intended to be, uniquely you. Create your own personal style, look, and vibe. Don't be afraid to be uniquely you. When you look at your personal style, what is it?

Start with how you dress, the way you style your hair, and how you do your makeup. Some of you might need a little help, and there is nothing wrong with asking. Reach out to a stylist to help you identify a way to define yourself through fashion. Create your authentic look and style. Next, hone in on signature effects like your scent, your handbags, your jewelry. If you're a man, focus on the way you wear your facial hair, your hats, your belts, and other unique styles.

Example

> I have a girlfriend who is known to always wear big, fun glasses. That is part of her authenticity. You would be shocked if you saw her without them or with basic glasses. You might not even recognize her.

What makes you special? We all have a gift, actually, many gifts. Our gifts are specific skills, talents, and abilities we are endowed with from birth or through life experiences. What are yours? You are probably wondering how to find them. Well, let's figure it out!

Some of you might be thinking, I don't know what my gifts are. Others might be thinking, I think I know what they are, and others yet might be totally tuned in and know right away what their gifts are. One way to find out what your gifts might be is to poll your friends and family. Ask them what they think your gifts and talents are. Family members can tell you what you have been good at since you were a child.

> Look through your belongings for clues. Some ideas to look at are the books you read and the magazines to which you subscribe. All the possessions and ideas that interest you are great indicators and can help point you in the right direction.

There are some great tools available to guide you on how to hone in on your specific strengths that make you who you are. The one I would like to recommend is the [1]CliftonStrengths assessment. You go online, take about thirty minutes to respond to questions, and get a report that outlines your specific strengths. What's interesting is how many traits there are and the order in which your traits fall into place. You can focus on your top five. It is rare to have anyone you know have the same top five and even rarer to have the same order of anyone's top five strengths.

The [2]Myers-Briggs Type Indicator is another popular tool to help you define your personality. This is another strength-finding assessment you can take. There is a lot of information online about this test.

How do you stand out in the crowd? What are your strengths that you want people to see? Don't be afraid to show off your skills when the opportunity arises. Confidence and a smile are two key elements of any successful person! Happy hunting and best of luck! I hope you have fun doing some research. There's so much joy to be found in figuring yourself out! Go get 'em, tiger!

[1]https://www.gallup.com/cliftonstrengths/en/252137/home.aspx
[2]https://www.myersbriggs.org/my-mbti-personality-type/mbti-basics/

Chapter 2

Education

It's Where You Learn

Picking the right school can make all the difference. Take your time and do your research, Start by doing some basic research on what makes a school a good choice. Learn the basics before you really dig in and start getting attached. The first item I would suggest you ask is if the school is accredited. Accreditation is an important topic in the interior design world.

DEFINITION
> Accreditation is the act of granting credit or recognition, especially to an educational institution that maintains suitable standards. Accreditation is necessary to any person or institution in education that needs to prove that they meet a general standard of quality.
> —Vocabulary.com Dictionary

You could start at one school and then have to move to another if it's not accredited. Then you might have to completely start over when you change schools. By start over, I mean none of your credits will transfer to the new school. Could you imagine? What a waste of time and money, right? I know several people who have had this happen to them.

When you try to get licensed or pass your National Council for Interior Design Qualification (NCIDQ), this is another time you will notice the accreditation importance come into play. The NCIDQ is an exam administered by the Council for Interior Design Qualification (CIDQ), which was incorporated in 1974. It is currently the only nationally recognized professional competency exam in the United States and Canada for interior designers.

Depending on what type of interior designer you decide to be will make a difference in how long you have to work for someone else who has met all the criteria. If you decide to go for your NCIDQ, you will need to work for someone who is NCIDQ accredited. This person will sign off and vouch for you and express your interior design work experience, once you meet all the time and experience requirements.

These are the education and work experience requirements as found on the CIDQ website.

EDUCATION
>Official education transcripts must include a minimum of sixty semester or ninety quarter credit hours of post-

secondary interior design coursework that encompasses a certificate, degree, or diploma from an accreditted institution to be eligible.

EXPERIENCE

Hours must be earned and affirmed by a Direct Supervisor and/or Sponsor. Up to 1,760 hours of interior design work experience, earned prior to graduation, may be included in overall work experience total.

—https://www.cidq.org/paths

Set yourself apart! Set your sights high!

Don't be afraid to go to the best school in your area. You are good enough! Apply yourself, put your heart into it, and don't be discouraged. One thing I have learned in life is that if you put your heart into something, nothing can stop you. If you don't get into the school you originally wanted, it's okay. You might find out later there was a reason for it. Don't doubt yourself. Make a decision and stick to it!

Most major cities will have several options for you to choose from, if you don't want to relocate. If you are open to relocation, don't hold back. Get online and look at all your options and apply to the schools that appeal to you the most!

Once you narrow your options, tour the schools. Hopefully, you can see into some classrooms in action. Request to see other areas you might spend a lot of time in, like the library, computer labs, and the cafeteria. Read reviews from multiple sources. Do not be afraid to ask questions. Unanswered questions can lead to uncertainty, and you don't want to be uncertain about your decision.

> If you want to go to school out of state, make sure to review tuition costs and living costs for out-of-state students. If you can go to the new state and live there for six months prior to enrolling in school, you might be able to get residency in the state. This could save you up to half the cost of being an out-of-state student. (Check requirements for your specific school of choice.)

Also, make sure to review any requirements to live on campus as part of your graduation requirements.

Example

My husband finished school at Ball State University with the number of credit hours needed to graduate. Upon applying for graduation, he was informed that he didn't meet the on-campus living requirement. He ended up having to go back to school, take random classes, and live on campus to check that box. His parents worked with a lawyer to try to allow him to graduate, but the school leaders wouldn't budge. They wanted him to live for an entire school year on campus, but in the end, they reduced it to half a year. He had found employment out of state and had already moved when he found this out. He had to move back to Indiana from Texas and put the job on hold. Thankfully, the new job was understanding.

Another important lesson I learned along the way, in the military, is that you don't have to wait until you get your diploma to become an interior designer. While you are in school or even before you start, you might know that you already are an interior designer. It is just a part of who you are, who you are meant to be. Own it! Be the interior designer you know you are. Getting the piece of paper at the end of your education will prove to the world that you earned your title. However, being an interior designer starts the moment you decide you are one. While in school, take it seriously, but don't forget this is a career of passion. Have fun with it. Don't stress about getting top grades and overdoing yourself. A bit of advice my mentor once told me was that nobody will ask you what grades you got in school. Let me tell you, this is so true! Nobody has ever asked me to see any of my grades.

Focus on learning and experiencing all the school is teaching and has to offer. Don't get me wrong, you should apply yourself and get good grades. I graduated with honors because I started this career later in life and wanted to prove I could excel and get honors. I took school slow and didn't max out on credit hours every semester, so I could enjoy the learning process. As the saying goes, "Take time to smell the roses."

Chapter 3

Volunteerism

It's Who You Help

Volunteerism is a great way to reach out to the community. What is more rewarding than helping others? When you volunteer, you get experience in exchange for helping someone in need. You will be surprised by how grateful the people you help will be. They will become your biggest advocates and help you out in the future. You can ask them to write testimonials for you, which you can use on your website and your social media accounts.

Don't forget to ask around to volunteer at places like your church, battered women shelters, the veterans community, or even community events. Don't forget to ask friends and family if they know of worthy causes for which you can volunteer.

Offering your services at functions that are doing silent auctions is another great way to give, to help raise funds for local charities. Volunteering is a great way to get some work under your belt when you are first getting started.

Tip

Offering to perform a service at low or no cost for the benefit of you learning from it is not only smart but thoughtful! For example, offer an interior design color consultation valued at $300 for a silent auction. Who knows? Once you get into their home and help them out, they might hire you to do more work, like update a few rooms!

Volunteering is a great way to get known. You never know who you could meet while volunteering and where the relationships you build could lead. Plus, you are helping someone else, which is awesome!

Example

Once I volunteered to give mini consultations at a local home show. I had a special banner and was considered a feature of the show, so I received extra attention. I set up a booth with a desk. People brought in floor plans and questions. I would sit down with them and answer their questions for ten minutes. I ended up getting several projects from the show. I was a feature on the local news station and many people said they saw me on TV and came right over. It was totally worth the time and effort involved.

Other ideas for community outreach are volunteering through different organizations, such as the American Society of Interior Designers (ASID), The International Design Association (IIDA), the International Foodservice Distributors Association (IFDA), the National Kitchen & Bath Association (NKBA), and the Network of Executive Women in Hospitality (NEWH), to name a few. Most organizations offer outreach programs.

The Arizona North Chapter of ASID, for example, does a yearly fundraiser called Interior Designer for Hire. There is a three-month window where the public can hire an interior designer, through the chapter, for a one- or two-hour consultation to help the purchaser with whatever he or she needs about interior design. This is a great way for the volunteer interior designer to get leads and the proceeds go to education and scholarships for the chapter. Once the interior designer visits the purchaser, the designer can assess the situation. If they are a good match, the designer could end up working for this new lead.

Volunteering has many benefits for both volunteers and receivers. While you offer services they couldn't perform themselves, you benefit by gaining confidence in a setting where your work is appreciated without money being involved. This is a win-win situation. You can also use this work to show others the projects you have completed and start building your portfolio.

Volunteering has many benefits. To find out about more opportunities, I suggest going online and doing a search on volunteering in your city. You will see there are a lot of opportunities for you to get out there and build a great reputation for yourself and network to make new connections!

Chapter 4

Mentorship

It's Who You Mentor and Who Mentors You

Mentorships are fundamental to your career. You don't want to go it alone. You will have questions along the way, trust me! Finding a good mentor is key. Make sure you think out what you would want in a mentor. Make a list of what you think would make a good mentor. What could you offer in return? Are you able to lend a hand for free to get in someone's door? Ask to shadow someone you think might be a good fit for you.

When you have the opportunity to work with a mentor without either person worrying about money or time, you can learn a lot. You will know right away if you enjoy being around the mentor, if he or she is a good teacher, is willing to share how to perform tasks, and if he or she is willing to introduce you to others.

What makes a good mentor?
- Someone you can, and would want to, strive to be in their shoes someday.
- Someone who has been successful in their career and can show you the ropes.
- Someone who has similar values and work ethic as you.
- Someone who teaches you about your career field.
- Someone you can go to with questions or problems when they arise. Believe me, quest-

ions will arise, and it is nice to have a friend in your corner when they do!
- Someone who can and wants to help you develop professionally.
- Someone who understands how to shine the light on someone besides themselves. Tip: When you shine the light on someone else, you, in turn, shine!

Be leery of people who will …
- use you.
- fail to share important learning points.
- default on training you on key matters.

Example

Someone who asks you to intern for experience (no money) and then doesn't teach you anything worthwhile. This person will have you doing personal errands, like picking up laundry. This person will not introduce you by name but instead will introduce you as a title (assistant, intern). This person will only ask you to do the busy work that he or she doesn't want to do.

A good mentor will introduce you to his or her contacts to help grow your network. Making the right connections in this industry is so important. If any of you are out on your own and have had to try to find contractors, you know what I am talking about. Having to try contractors out for the first time can be costly to you and your clients. When you use contractors you have met through your mentor who knows your knowledge level, it makes you look more seasoned. Being honest with the contacts you have formed from other contacts is key. You can have mentors everywhere.

Example

> John Doe, a tile guy you met from your mentor, knows you are just getting started. You say, "Hey, John, I have a new client. I would like you to come give me a quote." He knows you are going to need a little handholding. If he's a good mentor, then he will ask you all the right questions and will offer your clients clear explanations so you look good

because it is evident you have brought in an expert.

Meanwhile, you are learning yourself. The greatest part is your client has no idea. If you hire a random person, he might assume you know everything. If you don't ask for something, you don't get it, and your project can be less than it could be. Or even worse, your project could be missing some key element, like a shower niche in a bathroom remodel. Yikes!

Having a mentor helps you to learn industry best practices that you aren't taught in school. School does teach you a lot, however, there is a great number of on-the-job concepts it doesn't teach you. You will find out quickly that having someone to turn to, to answer questions, is important.

Chapter 5

Networking

It's Who You Know

When you go to networking events, do yourself a favor and put your shyness in the car and lock the door. Go into the event and shake hands, ask questions, figure out who's who. It's important who you associate with (societies, memberships).

Sign up for everything you can, until you see what you like the best. You will be pulled one way or another eventually. It's inexpensive to do this as a student, however, most societies offer discounts for students getting started as emerging professionals. This will save you lots of money in the long run! Attending events and getting your face out there will be vital.

Use any opportunity you have to volunteer to get involved deeper so you can make friends and learn the ins and outs of how business works. When you are looking for work, whose face are they going to remember? Y-O-U-R-S! People will remember you, so make sure you are memorable. (Remember to be authentically you. Refer to Chapter 1.)

Never burn a bridge—ever! If you have a falling out with someone, deal with it as professionally as possible. Even if that person is wrong. Always look at the bright side and keep your chin up. One thing

I have learned in life is that not everyone will appreciate you for your talents and uniqueness. You know what? That is okay. Those people aren't your people.

You never know which way life will take you and someone you might have never thought you would work with could make a decision if you get a job or not. Or even worse, he or she could be your next boss. (Could you imagine!?) So, no matter how you feel, be professional and don't let stress get the best of you.

Tip

When responding to hateful emails, wait until your blood pressure settles and there is little to no emotion involved. Write it in a separate document program, not in your email program, so you don't forget what you want to write and so you can thoughtfully and carefully craft your message without the worry of prematurely clicking "send." Go exercise to take your mind off of it or to vent a bit. Then reread it and edit it. Respond with a clear head. Once you send it, there is no going back. So, choose your words wisely. You can always read it to a close friend or a family member to make sure it is clear and that you aren't writing and sending a message you might regret in the future. Email is permanent and quickly shared.

Networking is an incredible way to grow your network, your business, and your friend base. Having your website, even if it's a simple landing page, up and running is important. There are many easy-to-use website builders online that you can build yourself for low cost.

Business cards are an absolute must, so people know how to contact you. As an interior designer, you do not need to put a physical address on your card. Adding your phone number, email address, and any associations you belong to are all great to put on your business card. If you attend a networking event at a show or a market, you will need a lot of cards, so plan accordingly. You want to be the one who shows up prepared.

Chapter 6

Work

It's Where You Work, Earn, and Learn

Don't be afraid to go for the big one. Set your sights high. You might start as a library keeper, however, at least you will learn where all the materials are located. When you get to that senior designer position, you know where to find everything. That means you will be faster and more competent when it comes to materials. When senior designers are in search of items, you will have all the answers. Who's getting promoted? Y-O- U!

When you go in for your interview, be prepared. Ask questions. Inquire about the company's culture. What does the company do as a team? Does it offer any team-building events? How is the overall morale?

> Ask around about the company beforehand. If you know any manufacturer representatives (from networking events) who call on the company, consult with them in regard to the overall culture and morale.

A good friend of mine said if an interior design firm treats the manufacturers' representatives poorly, you can only imagine how it treats the employees. I had no idea how right she was until I saw it with my own eyes.

Another step you should take is conduct online research and get to know everything you can about the company. Look for any reviews. Find out how many people have left the company and, if you can, try to find out why. If the company is known for a high turnover rate, there is a reason. Don't be so hungry for the job that you would put yourself in a bad situation.

Watch out for what my husband calls sweat shops! These are employers who expect you to keep your head down and hands on the keyboard. If the employees are afraid to talk or laugh, there is a reason.

There will be other job opportunities! You deserve to be treated with respect and dignity. Work isn't always a party, but you should be able to have some fun while working . . . right?

Other important considerations you should look for in employers are the following:

- Sufficient training — Do they offer any training for the position you are going after?

- Growth opportunities—Where do they see you in one year, three years, five years?
- Work-life balance—How do they feel about children, senior parents, or anyone who has special needs?

Benefits—Some of the main employee benefits are the following:

- Insurance: life, health, dental, vision
- Retirement: 401(k), matching
- Paid time off: observed holidays, personal time off (PTO), sick time, and vacation
- Flex working or teleworking: offers you the ability to work from home or different hours if needed
- Bonuses: performance and annual
- Student loan reimbursement
- Other educational opportunities
- Does the company volunteer?

Once you get the job, make sure there is respect and you feel valued. This is important! Remember that you are not stuck anywhere. There are always other opportunities to be had!

When one door closes, another one opens!

Chapter 7

Experience

It's Where You Get Your Hands Dirty!

Don't be afraid to get your hands dirty—you never know where that dirt will take you. I heard a well-known designer say she started by designing bathrooms and ended up doing the penthouse, along with many other rooms, in one of the largest, most well-known buildings in the world. Don't say, "It's just a bathroom," thinking that you want to work on a cool project, not bathrooms. You will. Be patient and give it time. Everyone has to start somewhere. Even starting with the bathrooms, in the largest building in the world, is darn awesome!

When you first start out, it's a beautiful thing. You get to see so many different styles. Soak up as much as you can, like a sponge. Keep your eyes and ears open. Touch everything. Ask questions, and don't pretend you know something if you don't.

It is okay not to know everything. It's expected. During this period, you have time to find what you enjoy and what your strengths are, what comes easy to you. You will start defining your own personal style. What makes you tick. What drives your passions. Then, roll with it!

A hard lesson to learn, especially if you are out on your own, is when to "say no." When you are out on your own, self-employed, you are eager to take on business. You are hungry. You want business, even if it's a bathroom. Ha, ha! There will be times when you will have to learn to say no and turn down projects that aren't in your wheelhouse.

Example

> If the project is craftsman style, and your design style is contemporary, you might not be the best person to do the job. It is absolutely okay to say to customers, "Sorry, this is not my style. To save you time and money, I have a friend I would love to refer you to." (If you do, of course!)

Explain your style to the clients and how it is different from what they want. If you fail to do so but take on the project, then you may show them design concepts they are not comfortable with, and it could turn into a struggle for you to get approval to move forward. Eventually, after wasting your client's time and project funds, the outcome would not be good for either of you. The last thing you want is a bad review. Be cautious and make decisions, following your instincts.

If you focus on your strengths and not your weaknesses, you can excel. You can specialize in your strengths and be really good at them. It won't feel like work. You will love being there, and your passion will show up in your work. You will feel excited, and so will your client!

Chapter 8

Strengths

It's What You're Good At

As discussed in Chapter 1, once you know your traits, you can focus on what you are naturally good at doing. So many people focus on the things they aren't good at. Isn't that a waste of time and energy?

Have you ever tried to improve in an area where you get a little better each time, but you don't see a huge improvement? It's because you were created differently and for different works. Let's focus on what we are good at, what comes easy to us. Why not be the best at what comes natural to you? You will be doing what you love, it will be easy for you, and, best of all, your passion will shine!

Stop spending energy on trying to be good at what other people are good at, just for the sake of competition. Some people are competitive and find themselves overexerting themselves, trying to learn a skill or a technique that comes really easily for a friend. For some reason, they don't excel in the same way. Why not just be happy for your friend who is good at whatever? Create your own lane and own it! Be good at being you!

Some strengths that don't have to do with your personality and can be instilled into you with discipline are reliability, punctuality, and accountability.

RELIABILTY

This trait is really important in the interior design field. Your clients, team members, and office mates will need to know if they can depend on you. So be confident, do what you say you will do, and follow through. Reliability is one of the most important strengths I look for when working with others.

PUNCTUALITY

Being on time shows you are excited to be where you are and that you are taking the project seriously. When you are dealing with a team of construction members, you do not want to waste their time. In our industry, time is money. If they are waiting for you, they aren't working. It takes away the time they have allotted for the project. If your clients are there waiting and see you are keeping everyone waiting, it makes you look really bad. This is their money everyone is spending.

Tip

If you have difficulty being on time, set your appointments a half hour before you have to be there to trick yourself into being on time! Plan ahead, set your clothes out the night before, pack your things, and put them close to your door so you can grab and go!

ACCOUNTABILY

Be responsible to your clients and those you work with. If you are going to be late because of an accident or a flat tire or other unforeseen event, call right away. Let everyone know you might need to reschedule. Sometimes others are in the same boat as you and will appreciate the heads-up. Other times, you will be able to allow them to take more time to do what they need to do and arrive at a later planned time. This is the professional way to handle it.

Find your strengths and use them to the best of your ability. You will look great doing what you are naturally good at! Don't forget to follow professional courtesy, and you will be at the top of your game!

Chapter 9

Recognition

It's Where You Get Noticed

Awards, Getting Published, As Seen In!

When it comes to getting recognized, this goes back to networking. If you are involved in an association or society, you will have access to awards. Usually these are held yearly. Most times, you have to pay a small fee to enter and have to purchase a ticket to attend. Look for smaller, local events and competitions to get practice and to get your name out there. You might just win!

When you complete a project you think is worthy of an award, you should enter it! Don't be afraid to enter into the awards competition. The experience alone is worth it! When you are putting your submissions together, read and follow all the instructions. If you don't have every piece needed, your entry will be disqualified. So be meticulous and review and doublecheck everything. Be clear and concise in your statements and make sure if you talk about your project, the image you are presenting shows it and vice versa.

If you don't win, do not let it get you down. Keep entering and try again.

Tip

Volunteer to judge the awards for others. This way you know what it's like to be a judge and see what the judges are looking for. This will help your submissions tremendously in the future.

PHOTOGRAPHY

Spend the money on professional photographers who are well-known in your interior design community. (Ask your mentor for a good contact.) Professional photographers know what they are doing—that's why there is a big price tag. Pay it. Do not try to shortcut and do your own photos (I know our smartphones take awesome photos) or have your family photographer do them. Yes, I tried both of these options. They failed, just like you wouldn't go to a plumber for a root canal. Use a professional. You won't be sorry.

GETTING PUBLISHED

Get to know editors of local magazines. They will call on you in a time of need to fill issues. Don't be afraid to email your latest work to them. If they don't use them, don't give up. They eventually will. Try to create relationships. Nurture your relationships so they remember you. This goes back to your networking skills we talked about in Chapter 5.

Chapter 10

Communication

It's How You Express Yourself

Everyone will tell you that communication is key. It is so true. There are many parts of communication, and I will touch on some of my favorites. You will find out over time what works best for you.

Listening is a process, and there are several techniques for active listening. If you haven't researched active listening, you should. It's really interesting. When you are listening to your clients, make sure you use a method I call BET!

> B—Be present.
> E—Engage with eye contact.
> T—Take notes.

BE PRESENT
When you are present, you are aware of your surroundings. You are focused and intent on the matter at hand. Keep your mind clear, so you can pay attention to your meeting with your clients. Be calm. Stay away from stimulants like caffeine before a meeting, so you can stay calm and soak in information. If you are easily agitated, you might get distracted if you are caffeinated or hyper.

ENGAGE WITH EYE CONTACT
When you talk to people, look them in their eyes and try to connect with them. Take time to pause and

truly listen to what they're saying. Don't look around, and don't be shifty. Just pretend you are talking to a peer and be yourself. Look for ways you can connect to them and be memorable. Being yourself is the one thing that sets you apart from everyone else. Be authentically you!

TAKE NOTES

Clients love to see you taking notes; you look prepared and professional. It shows you care about what they are saying so much that you want to capture it in the moment. You are diligent and want to get all the information they are giving you. When you don't take notes, you could possibly forget or miss an important detail such as their kid's name or where they want the outlet for their blow dryer.

> When you take good notes, you can refer to them later. If there are any questions on how you managed the project, you will also have a record of the conversations and requests.

In your notes, you can also add details, sketches, and diagrams. Making a sketch for your clients to see, on the spot, shows you are understanding their design ideas. For example, you can sketch out a floor or wall design for a shower remodel to know where the clients would like the plumbing fixtures or the shampoo niche or a bench. It is a great way to make sure you are all on the same page. It's crucial to take notes; trust me . . . don't learn the hard way! It would be embarrassing to have to go back and say, "Sorry, I didn't take note of your desires, and I don't recall them either. Would you mind telling me again?"

Body language is another favorite way to communicate! When you are actively listening, you should have good posture—two feet on the ground and look into your client's eyes when you aren't taking notes. Don't cross your arms or legs. Crossing parts of your body is not inviting. Don't tap fingers or pens on surfaces; it is distracting. Try to not touch your face or hair; don't overthink it.

Pay attention to your proximity to the clients. Are they comfortable being close to you, or do they back away? If you are sitting at a table, do not put your elbows on the table and don't hold up your head in your hand. This makes you look bored. Hand gestures also say a lot about how the conversation is going. If your clients have their hands in their pockets or keep touching their hair, it could mean they are nervous and need some reassurance.

HOW TO SAY "NO"

There will be times in your career when you will have to say no. It is okay to say no. It isn't easy in the beginning, however, it is necessary. Saying no is an interesting way of showing your confidence. You are showing you know what you won't do. Your instincts will guide you in most situations, but in some cases, you might need to turn to your mentor for some solid advice.

Some clients will ask you for the impossible. Some clients will ask you to do a bunch of work for nothing; not cool. By the way, you do not owe your family or your friends anything. Don't burden yourself with helping friends in times where you are better off making money. Remember the phrase "No good deed goes unpunished."

One of the most common requests I get from clients is "Can your team have this done in two weeks?" Unfortunately, people all too often wait until the last minute to hire you, and then somehow it becomes your issue to try to jump through hoops to give them what they need.

Tip

Never commit on the spot. Respond with "I will need to confer with all the contractors involved to see how their schedules look, and I will get back to you." Once you get the hang of it, you will be saying "no" and feeling good about it before you know it!

Chapter 11

Positivity

It's How to Ensure You're On!

Positivity just comes natural to some people! Let's face it; for some others, it takes a lot of effort! When you are working with clients, no matter what is going on in your life, you should be what I call "ON"! You should be happy and enjoyable to be around. It is not their concern, nor should you waste their time with your personal issues or problems. Keep it business, and keep it on!

If you have worked with a client on more than one occasion and have built a personal rapport with him or her, you might be able to add some small talk about your family, if asked. However, diving into your personal life is not businesslike. You need to remember you are there to make money and keep the client's trust in you and your ability to take care of his or her needs.

Positivity is infectious too! When you are positive, people around you pick up on your vibe. The same goes for negativity. If you have trouble being positive, here are some suggestions that can help you be upbeat when you are about to hop on a call or drive to see a client.

- Listen to your favorite songs (especially songs that make you feel powerful)! Mine is "Confident" by Demi Lovato.

- Meditate for a few minutes on all the things you are grateful for in your life.
- Practice breathing exercises to take more oxygen to your brain.
- If you have time, work out or go for a quick walk. Exercise is a natural stimulant.
- Make sure you are well fed! Grab a favorite snack on the way out the door if you are in a rush!

Be infectious! Positivity breeds more positivity. When you are with clients and you are on, it is going to instill more trust in you. They are happy to see you and enjoy your company and, in turn, will give you their trust. On the other hand, if you are wavering and not in a good mood, you might set them off, and they could seem uneasy, making them feel like they don't know what is going on. You've got this!

Chapter 12

Relatability

It's When You Put Yourself in Their Shoes ... Not Literally, of Course!

Being relatable is a great characteristic, in my opinion. Having the ability to understand what your clients are experiencing is a huge advantage. Some points to ponder are these. Have you ever gone through a remodel? Have you ever lived without the use of your kitchen or bathroom? It can be a dusty mess that seems to never end!

Listen carefully to your clients. Don't forget to take notes and speak their language. Repeat back to them their thoughts and ideas and make sure they get it. Make sure you are up front with your clients about the transition to their new awesome space. They are looking to you as their expert to rely on—a professional who can relate to their experience.

Do not ever make excuses. You should be honest. Sometimes challenges come up, and you just have to deal with them. Don't sugarcoat it. If you make it sound like no big deal and it is, you will lose their trust. Homes age, and things happen—mold, water damage, cracks in the foundation, movement of the foundation—all kinds of unwelcome surprises over which you and your team obviously have no control. However, you and your team can assist on getting them repaired. So, if these types of issues come up, don't fret. Be honest and let the clients know there will be a change order to repair and move on.

Remember, if you are doing residential interior design, you are in their home, touching their personal belongings. Sometimes, you are in their personal spaces and touching their incredibly personal possessions. Keep that at the top of your mind all the time.

Some interesting objects I have had to handle include pet remains, stuffed real animals (yes, real ones), and expensive Hermès china (on the top rung of a ladder in a pantry—I thought I might die of anxiety). These are moments my mentor and great friend and I still crack up about! You honestly never know! Be prepared, and don't look shocked!

> I always tell my team to act like there are cameras and speakers everywhere. Do not do anything that you wouldn't want your client to see on a video. Do not talk about the client until you are away from the home. It is professional decency.

Chapter 13

Protection

It's How You Put Safeguards in Place

As one of my favorite college professors used to say to us, "CYA—cover your assets!"

When you are in someone's home, anything can happen. You could step on their beloved Fifi or accidentally drop a vase from Grandma Verna who is no longer with us—bless her soul. Make sure you carry sufficient insurance to cover your team and yourself while on the job. If you are working with others, make them provide you with a copy of their insurance before they step foot on a project. Make sure they aren't a liability.

EXPECTATIONS
You are their expert, like I said earlier. The clients are counting on you to provide them with guidance and all the information regarding the project. Let them know upfront the steps you and your team will be taking. Outline it in your contract. As the project advances, you can remind them what stage is coming up next.

You also need to instill in them that you surround yourself with other professionals and you trust them, so they should too. Don't waiver in decision-making. Exude confidence. If you don't know how to perform a task, figure it out. You can always say something along the lines of, "Let me do a little research and get back to you on that one."

CONTRACTS

All professionals should have a proper contract or a letter of agreement. Do not start a project without one, period. Professional associations have them for purchase. You should learn about them in school. Bottom line is you need to write out what you think the expectations are.

I create a list of the design processes and put dates by them as I go along to keep myself in check. It is a great way to stay organized and on track with your plan of action.

This is what I use.

> I propose the following services:
>
> ### I. Programming and Research
> Interview
> Inventory
> Measure the spaces to prepare accurate floor plans
> Verify site conditions
> Develop project schedule
> Meeting for revision and approval

II. Schematic Design
Preliminary space plan and inspiration plans
Preliminary furniture plans
Preliminary specifications
Preliminary budget
Meetings for review and approval

III. Design Development
Finalize floor plan
Finalize specifications
Finalize budget
Meeting for review and approval

IV. Contract Documents
Qualify vendors
Meeting for review and approval

V. Contract Administration
Procure furniture, fixtures, and equipment (FF&E)
Site visits and inspections
Meetings with client
Project finalization and evaluation

BILLING
You will need to have the compensation breakdown. How do you want to get paid for this project? Are

you billing by the hour or is there a flat fee for the project? I find that some clients prefer a flat fee so they aren't concerned about how much time you are spending talking to them or looking at things.

You can average out how many hours you think you will take to do the project, add a little cushion, and come up with a fee. Or you can do a by-the-square-footage fee based on what you think is best for you. If you are super busy, hourly might be the best option so your clients are staying on their toes, timewise, and not wasting your time. It really depends on what works best for you.

You will need to have the legal jargon and information for the project. It goes something like this.

> Other terms and conditions applicable to this project.
>
> - Warehousing, delivery, and freight charges will be charged with the final bill once the fees are understood.
> - Drawings and documents prepared for this project remain the property of the interior designer and cannot

be used without permission of the designer.
- With your permission, the designer would like to take photographs of the space before and after and use them for publishing.
- The designer provides good faith in assisting you in obtaining the services of qualified contractors but cannot be held responsible for the performance, quality, or timely completion of work by these third parties.
- The designer can provide on-site supervision if any contractors are present, if requested.
- Any work that the client requests of the interior designer in addition to the work described will only be started after an amended agreement has been prepared and approved by both parties.
- Either party might terminate this agreement at any time. In the event of termination by the client, the client agrees to pay the designer for all work completed up to the time of termination.

- The client and designer agree that this letter constitutes the complete agreement between the designer and the client.
- Both parties also agree that disputes are to be handled by a third-party arbitrator.

If you have a lawyer you can talk to about setting up your contract, it's a good idea. As you continue to work with clients, over time you will find other points to add to your contract.

Chapter 14

Workbook

It's What Inspires, Drives, and Motivates You to Be the Best You Can Be in Interior Design

I have three questions for you. Research your answers and really dig deep. Don't hold back. What are your biggest dreams? My mom always says, "You can accomplish anything if you put your heart into it."

Answer the following questions.

- What inspires, drives, motivates me to be the best that I can possibly be?
- Why do I want to be an interior designer?
- What is my dream job and why?

After you have your answers to these three questions, make a list of 100 reasons why.

Example

I want to help people.
I want to design beautiful spaces.
I want to work for a big firm.
I want to own my own business.
I want to travel.

When you make your list, you will have these items to look back on.

I like to do a little meditation or prayer time before I go to bed and when I wake. I look over my list and imagine myself doing what I love. When you are doing this, imagine yourself as if it has already happened. What are you doing? Where are you? What feelings are you feeling? Feel those feelings!

This tool will help you to manifest and make your dreams and goals come true. Remember, look back on your list from time to time and be grateful for all the goals as they come true. A song, "The Climb" by Miley Cyrus, comes to mind. Be prepared to be amazed! Enjoy the journey!

Try to remember that your struggles are still steps forward. You might not see it for what it is worth during the struggle. However, it will come to light before you know it. Don't ever give up on your dreams and keep moving forward!

Best of luck on your adventure!

XO, Tabitha

About the Author

Award-winning interior designer Tabitha Evans is an established and well-respected member of the interior design industry. She is the principal interior designer of Tabitha Evans Design, a design studio based in Arizona. Tabitha is married and has three children, a dog, and a tortoise. When she is not designing, she loves traveling, cooking, gardening, and fashion.

Tabitha believes interior design is fundamental; it transforms lives. She believes interior design can impact your health, and she wants you to feel great in your space. She believes in humanizing the living, working, and healing environments and is passionate about what she does!!

As a member and past-president (2017-2018) of the Arizona North Chapter of the American Society of Interior Design (ASID), she loves volunteering and giving back to the community. Currently, she holds the title of Government Affairs Representative to the Board for the Arizona North Chapter of the American Society of Interior Design (ASID). She has been awarded with several prestigious awards and has been published in magazines locally, regionally, and nationally.

Tabitha attended school at the Art Institute of Phoenix where she graduated with honors with a Bachelor of Arts in Interior Design. Tabitha is an innovator, creator, and visionary. She believes, through collaboration and communication from everyone who will use the space, the outcome of the design will be something truly special.

Tabitha is also a veteran of the United States Army. She spent over six years as a signals intelligence analyst. Tabitha Evans' designs are influenced by her extensive world travels. She has lived in Asia, Europe, and the United States. Her current mission, outside of interior design, is mentoring others so they can learn from their trials, and she helps them see all of the great opportunities before them.

www.ingramcontent.com/pod-product-compliance
Lightning Source LLC
Chambersburg PA
CBHW071009080526
44587CB00015B/2397